BRITANNICA BEGINNER B

W9-AWW-798

HILLARY CLINTON
AMERICA'S MOST INFLUENTIAL FEMALE POLITICIAN

JEFF MAPUA

Britannica
Educational Publishing

IN ASSOCIATION WITH

ROSEN
EDUCATIONAL SERVICES

Published in 2015 by Britannica Educational Publishing (a trademark of Encyclopædia Britannica, Inc.) in association with The Rosen Publishing Group, Inc.
29 East 21st Street, New York, NY 10010

Distributed exclusively by Rosen Publishing.
To see additional Britannica Educational Publishing titles, go to rosenpublishing.com.

First Edition

Britannica Educational Publishing
J.E. Luebering: Director, Core Editorial Group
Mary Rose McCudden: Editor, Britannica Student Encyclopedia

Rosen Publishing
Hope Lourie Killcoyne: Executive Editor
Jacob R. Steinberg: Editor
Nelson Sá: Art Director
Brian Garvey: Designer
Cindy Reiman: Photography Manager
Karen Huang: Photo Researcher

Library of Congress Cataloging-in-Publication Data

Mapua, Jeff.
Hillary Clinton/Jeff Mapua.—First edition.
        pages cm.—(Britannica Beginner Bios)
Includes bibliographical references and index.
ISBN 978-1-62275-689-6 (library bound) — ISBN 978-1-62275-690-2 (pbk.) — ISBN 978-1-62275-691-9 (6-pack)
1. Clinton, Hillary Rodham—Juvenile literature. 2. Presidents' spouses—United States—Biography—Juvenile literature.
3. Women legislators—United States—Biography—Juvenile literature. 4. United States. Congress. Senate—Biography—Juvenile literature. 5.
Women politicians—United States—Biography—Juvenile literature. 6. Women presidential candidates—United States—Biography—Juvenile
literature. 7. Women cabinet officers—United States—Biography—Juvenile literature. I. Title.
E887.C55M36 2015
327.730092—dc23
[B]
                                                                                                              2014015673

Manufactured in the United States of America

CONTENTS

CHAPTER ONE

MEET HILLARY CLINTON

Hillary Rodham Clinton is a famous United States politician. A politician is someone who is active in the government. Hillary Clinton was a United States senator and secretary of state. She also served as the First Lady while her husband, Bill Clinton, was president. The wife of the president is called the First Lady.

First Lady

Bill Clinton became president in 1993. The White House then

Hillary Clinton has had many jobs, including secretary of state.

became their home and office. Hillary set up her own office in the White House. As First Lady, she wanted everyone to have good health care. She tried to pass laws that would make it easier for everyone to receive health care.

Senator

At the end of her time as First Lady, Hillary was elected

Quick Fact

Hillary campaigned with her husband, Bill Clinton. This means she gave speeches and talked with voters. She helped Bill become the president of the United States.

Hillary was already an active politician when her husband, Bill, was president.

to the U.S. Congress. Congress is the branch of government that makes laws. There are two groups in Congress.

One group is called the House of Representatives. The other group is called the **SENATE**. In 2000 Hillary was elected a senator for the state of New York.

Secretary of State

In 2009, Hillary left her job as senator to become the secretary of state for President Barack Obama. The secretary of state leads the Department of State. This department handles the United States' dealings with other countries. For that job Hillary made hundreds of trips around the world to meet with foreign leaders.

The **SENATE** is one of the two groups in the U.S. Congress. Congress makes laws.

The U.S. Capitol is in Washington, D.C.

CHAPTER TWO

EARLY LIFE

Hillary Diane Rodham was born on October 26, 1947. She grew up in a city near Chicago, Illinois. Her father, Hugh, was a business owner. Her mother, Dorothy, was a stay-at-home mom. Hillary worked

Hillary is shown here in her high school yearbook photo.

hard in school. She became interested in politics as a teenager.

Education

In 1965 Hillary went to Wellesley College in Massachusetts. She studied government and politics. At this time, many people in the United States worked for women and African Americans to have more rights. Hillary believed in those efforts. She soon joined the **DEMOCRATIC PARTY.**

After graduating from college, Hillary went to Yale Law School. There she became interested in family law. Family law deals with topics such as marriage, divorce, and adoption. Hillary was also interested in other areas that can affect children, such

The **DEMOCRATIC PARTY** is one of the two main political parties in the United States. A political party is a group of people who have similar ideas about how the government should act. They try to influence or direct the government.

as health care. She earned her law degree in 1973.

Meeting Bill Clinton

Hillary met Bill Clinton when they were both law students. They met at the school library. Hillary saw Bill looking at her from across the room. She walked over to say hello. Bill was very nervous when they met. He later said he even forgot his own name!

Hillary studied at Wellesley College.

After graduation, Bill moved to Arkansas to teach law at the University of Arkansas. Hillary took a job in Washington, D.C., but it

9

soon ended. In 1974 she decided to move to Arkansas to be with Bill. She also taught law at the University of Arkansas.

In 1974, Bill ran in an election for Congress. Hillary helped him with his campaign, but Bill lost that race.

On October 11, 1975, they got married. Bill became attorney general of Arkansas, and they

Before he became president of the United States, Bill Clinton was the governor of Arkansas.

Quick Fact

Hillary Clinton became a teacher at the University of Arkansas when she was only 27 years old. She was the same age as many of her students!

moved to Little Rock, the state capital. In 1978 Bill was elected the governor of Arkansas. That means he was the leader of that state.

First Lady of Arkansas

In Little Rock, Hillary became an important lawyer. She was the first female lawyer at her law firm. In 1980 Bill and Hillary had a daughter named Chelsea. Bill lost his job as governor of Arkansas in 1981, but he was reelected in 1982.

While Bill Clinton was the governor of Arkansas, Hillary worked on many issues concerning children. One of her goals was to make schools better. She believed that giving children a good education was necessary. The people of Arkansas agreed. Bill Clinton

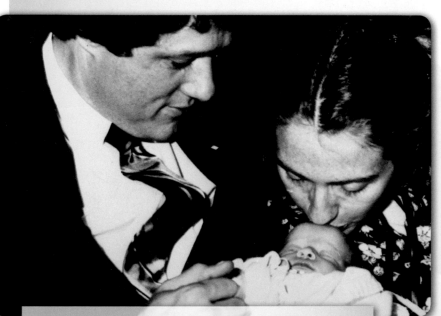

Bill and Hillary Clinton hold their baby daughter, Chelsea.

In 2013, Hillary visited a new children's library in Little Rock, Arkansas, that was named after her.

Quick Fact

Hillary Clinton was named one of the nation's 100 most influential lawyers in 1988 and 1991.

became a very popular governor. People began to think that he could be the next president of the United States.

CHAPTER THREE

THE FIRST LADY

In 1992 Bill Clinton ran for president of the United States. Hillary supported her husband in his campaign. Some people thought that Hillary would hurt Bill's chances of winning the election. Many people did not like how much she influenced Bill's decisions.

However, Hillary helped her husband become the president. She gave him a lot of advice. She also gave speeches during his campaign. She went on television with him. After Bill became president, Hillary set up her own office in the White House.

When her husband, Bill, ran for president, Hillary was there to help his campaign.

Health Care

As First Lady, Hillary wanted to improve **HEALTH CARE** in the country. One problem was

HEALTH CARE is keeping the body and mind healthy, especially by visiting doctors and taking medicine.

that many people could not afford to go to a doctor when they were sick. Hillary wanted to make sure everyone in the country could pay for doctor and hospital visits.

She came up with a plan to improve health care for Americans. She wanted to make it a law, but

Hillary Clinton stood at her husband's side on the day he became president of the United States.

first it had to be approved by Congress. She fought for it very hard, but in the end Congress turned down her idea.

Families First

Hillary continued to fight hard for the rights of others. She fought for children's

Hillary spoke to many different groups about women's rights and other issues.

rights when she was a lawyer. She also believed that men and women should have the same rights and be treated equally. In 1995 Hillary gave a speech in Beijing, China. She said, "Human rights are women's rights… and women's rights are human rights." She wanted women everywhere to have full access to education, health care, and jobs.

In 2001 Bill reached the end of his time as president. Now it was his turn to support Hillary.

CHAPTER FOUR

REACHING NEW HEIGHTS

Hillary was offered many jobs when her time as First Lady was coming to an end. She was asked to run companies and to teach at a college. However, Hillary decided to run for Congress. Bill gave Hillary a lot of help. They bought a home in New York. In 1999 she became a **CANDIDATE** for a seat in the U.S. Senate for the state of New York.

The campaign was hard. The other candidate was a Republican named Rick Lazio. Lazio was from New York, but Hillary had just moved there. Hillary went around the state and met local New Yorkers. Her efforts paid off! Hillary won the 2000 election.

In 2000, Hillary ran for Congress against Rick Lazio.

A **CANDIDATE** is somebody who runs in an election or is proposed for an office or honor.

19

Hillary the Senator

Hillary worked hard to earn the respect of her fellow senators. She was a dedicated and hard-working senator. Just like when she was First Lady, Hillary fought to make health care better. The people of New York liked Hillary as their senator. She was easily reelected in 2006.

Quick Fact

Hillary Clinton was still the First Lady when she was elected to the Senate in 2000.

Race for the Presidency

In 2007 Hillary announced that she would run for president in 2008. She was a popular candidate. However, Senator Barack Obama won the Democratic **NOMINATION**. Obama went on to win the

When a person receives their political party's NOMINATION, it means he or she is chosen as their candidate for an election.

Like her husband, Hillary Clinton also ran for president of the United States.

presidential election. He chose Hillary to be his secretary of state.

Secretary of State

The secretary of state is in charge of the Department

Hillary was secretary of state for President Barack Obama.

of State. This department helps the United States work with other countries. The secretary of state travels to other countries and makes deals with them. Hillary made hundreds of trips around the world. She met with the leaders of many countries.

CHAPTER FIVE

THE FUTURE

Many people praised Hillary Clinton's work as secretary of state. She worked hard to make the United States' relationships with other countries stronger. She left the position in 2013.

Part of her job as secretary of state required Hillary to travel around the world.

Quick Fact

Hillary Clinton was replaced as secretary of state by John Kerry. Before that, John Kerry was a senator from Massachusetts, where Hillary went to college.

When Hillary left her job as secretary of state in 2013, John Kerry took over her position.

The Clinton Foundation

When Hillary was a senator, Bill Clinton started a charity. He named it the Clinton Foundation. The Clinton Foundation helps people around the world. One of the charity's biggest interests is the **ENVIRONMENT**. It also supports human rights and health care. In 2013 the name was changed to the Bill, Hillary & Chelsea Clinton Foundation. That same year, Hillary began a project for the foundation called "No Ceiling: The Full Participation